HIS HEART
My Hand

Poetry in The Spirit

Deehna R. Busby

PRESS

Dedications

This work is dedicated first and foremost
to the Master Craftsman who spoke it
into existence, breathed upon it by His
Spirit, and has made Himself transparent
and open to the world through its pages.
Father GOD, you have amazed me once
again! I am honored and privileged to
serve You as one of your present-day
Kingdom scribes!
Be Glorified in me!

This work is also dedicated to the body
of Christ...the Blood-bought family
of believers, who oftentimes need
encouragement to finish strong for GOD,

no matter what the circumstance or the cost. We are all in this together. In these last and evil days, we need each other like never before...

Iron sharpens Iron.

This work is finally dedicated to my friends who have yet to come into the fullness of Christ. I write that you might know that you are loved beyond compare. There is nothing you can do, say, attempt, or think to cause GOD'S Love for you to diminish. As a matter of fact, He so loves you, that He has made a way for you to be with Him forever...through His Darling Son, Jesus the CHRIST. My hope and prayer for you is that somewhere, lodged within these pages, you find the message that pricks your heart to ask the question, "What must I do to be saved?"

He is waiting for you, dear one!

Contents

- *Introduction*.................................. **ix**
- *Write The Word*................................ 18
- *A Servant Of GOD*............................. 21
- *I'm Persuaded To Follow Thee* 24
- *Answer The Master's Call* 27
- *In The Waiting* 30
- *No Greater Love*............................... 33
- *O Lord*... 36
- *Be At Peace*...................................... 39
- *You, GOD, You*.................................. 42
- *Oh, To Be Kept By Jesus*.................... 45
- *Persevere* 48
- *Do You Have Access To The King?*..... 51

- *Family*.. 55
- *I See Myself Again*............................. 58
- *I Would Be Insane, Lord*.................... 63
- *Make GOD Your Home Page*............... 67
- *Picture This*... 70
- **What's In A Name?**....................... **75**
- *I Live Because Mama Prayed*............. 78
- *Prophetic Gift You Are*........................ 81
- *Daughter of My Holiness*.................... 87
- *Rose*.. 93
- *Let Them See* 97
- *My Love For You* 102
- *Mercy To Me* 107
- *Young Man*... 111
- *Ode To Randy*.................................... 115
- **A Special Note About**
  Our Children.............................. **117**
- *A Child's Prayer Declaration* 122

Introduction

How do I love thee? Let me count the ways.

It was early in my life that GOD arrested me with His Love. The Bible came alive to me while I was a child. I loved to read, so that helped. The Webster's Dictionary, The World Book Encyclopedia, and The Holy Bible, became the foundational elements for my unquenchable thirst for knowledge, and my undying love for words and their meanings. I just could not get enough. I would read, then think about what I read, then write about what I read.

During my teen years, I struggled with self-esteem and self-concept issues. Even though I was friendly, many times I felt isolated from the crowd. I didn't talk like the others. I viewed and valued things differently. I seemed to have understanding and wisdom way beyond my years. Yet, all I really wanted was to fit in somehow. Not to be laughed at because I was thin was a major daily hope of mine. The deep feelings of unworthiness would force me to write about what I could share with no one. No one, that is, but GOD.

At age 17, something beautiful happened to me. GOD had seen my *"growing pains"*, had evidently read all of my "love notes" to HIM, and chose this time in my life to bring together my interest in words, my experiences growing up, and my love for Him. What a unique blend! I found out that day, back at that California church, just how much GOD really loved me! It was like He lifted me out of the congregation, visited with me, told me secrets, kissed and hugged on me, and showed me a side of Himself I never knew before. I cried and felt so happy for what seemed like days. It was sheer euphoria-I now had an experience that would top all other experiences I'd ever had. I, Deehna Rachelle Hall, had been out in the Spirit-on a date with The Almighty GOD! *So there!*

I will never forget what the Lord told me on that day. His poetic style of sharing made me believe every Word He said. I easily resonated with His whispers of love.

It was as if The Master Poet Himself was giving me tips on how to share His Heart with those who He hand-picked to receive His *Heart Message.* What an honor to be in the *actual* presence of the One True GOD-and He *actually* let some drops fall on me!

Between the tears and laughter, I tried to compose myself. But something had hold of me! Just writing these lines puts me in remembrance of every emotion I experienced while in the Throne Room with Him. GOD pulled me in to Him, and drew me to my knees in humble adoration of Who He is, What He's done, Where He inhabits, When He shows up, Why He loves me, and How He's made a way for me to live...free from the guilt, shame, and embarrassment of the past.

That was the beginning of a lifetime of precious moments and dances I've had with GOD. Over the years, I've recorded so many stories and poems...all illustrating His outpourings and teachings to me about His Creation, His Children, His Word, His World, and much, much more. I regret that much of what was written has been lost, except for that which lies in my heart. However, the Handwriter on the wall has brought revival and newness to this present-day Kingdom scribe!

As I continue to live out His Plan for me, I am able to see more and more clearly how much unconditional love The Father has for His children-you and I. He calls us all to Himself so we can experience the joy and peace that He is so willing and ready to give us. Our Holy Creator is waiting for you...whoever you are. He wants to share His Heart with you. You have become an attraction to HIM...He sees you right where you are, and He has a right-now Word for you. My hope is that as you read this book, that Our Savior will breathe upon you... and you will be caught up in The Lord's Refrain...His *poetry in the spirit.*

Enjoy

The

Journey!

drb

Dedicated to:

The Habakkuk 2 writers...

Then the Lord answered me and said:
"Write the vision and make it
plain on tablets,
That he may run who reads it."
Habakkuk 2:2

WRITE THE WORD

Write the vision, make it plain!
And record the Lord's refrain

Take those Words from up above
And script them with a heart of love

Choose the Words that bring new life
And still the envy, greed and strife

Put forth the message pure again
And let God's voice be heard in them

Don't stop writing, Saint of GOD
The Holy Hope of our great Lord

The **Divine Diary**, His Heart-Your Hand
The **Noble Notes**, His Thoughts-Your Stand

Whatever He says, Don't miss a word
Some life is forging by that sword

May come at night, May come by day
Expect the Word to come your way

Ascribe GOD'S Law, His Word let be
So men can read attentively

And live thereby and be made whole
Those who follow the **Spiritual Scrolls**

The **Christ Chronicles**, Make known
His case
How Jesus came to save the human race

And point all Heaven's prospects to Thee
By the **Justified Journal** of GOD Almighty

For:

The Race Runners...

To those who realize what the true

prize looks like!

"For to me, to live is Christ,

and to die is gain".

Philippians 1:21

A SERVANT OF GOD

To be a servant of GOD is my truest desire

To run like His Wind and to fight
like His Fire

To live how He wants and never to tire

To trudge if He wills through the muck
and the mire

When the enemy pushes me into the briars

I will press towards the mark, forget
anything prior

I will speak in His stead, be His Kingdom
Town Crier

And say, "God is the Truth, satan you
are the liar

Let my life tell His story, Be a Heavenly Flyer

For GOD is my boss and I am His hire

Leaving no room for doubt, Let's get down
to the wire

Since GOD is my King, my response is
"Yes, Sire"!

To:

The Servant-Followers...

Who have made Christ their Leader

at all costs!

Then a certain scribe came and

said to Him,

"Teacher, I will follow you

wherever you go."

Matthew 8:19

I'M PERSUADED TO FOLLOW THEE

Along this narrow soldier's road
I'm persuaded to follow Thee.
In this life of to and fro
I'm persuaded to follow Thee.
When trails turn and valleys appear
And when the threat of death is near
When cloudy days seem not to clear
I'm persuaded to follow Thee.

As I travel on the paths before
I'm persuaded to follow Thee.
When closed becomes the open door
I'm persuaded to follow Thee.
When happiness seems to be on loan
Friends are gone and I'm all alone
And deep inside there's an ache and a groan
I'm persuaded to follow Thee.

At times, the load seems hard to bear
I'm persuaded to follow Thee.
The garment of praise seems heavy to wear
I'm persuaded to follow Thee.
As cries go up and laughs are few
And no relief is in my view
I'll tell you what my heart will do
I'm persuaded to follow Thee.

As darkness tries to hide the light
I'm persuaded to follow Thee.
When prayer's the only way to fight
I'm persuaded to follow Thee.
If all becomes lost as I press through
If holding on means breaking, too
For my decrease brings Glory to You
I'm persuaded to follow Thee.

Dedicated To:

The Procrastinators...

Who know they've been called

to Kingdom work-

May the "*buck*" stop here!

For you see your calling, brethren, that not

many wise according to the flesh, not many

mighty, not many noble, are called.

1 Corinthians 1:26

ANSWER THE MASTER'S CALL

How does one answer The Master's Call?
Do you pray, then wait 'til the fire falls
Do you sit quietly, doing nothing at all?
Do you stand and turn your face
to the wall?

Do you enter your closet, then
close the door?
Or maybe you lie prostrate on the floor?
Perhaps you shout to the top
of your voice?
Or is singing a song your wait of choice?

I know-I'll meet with my best friend!
Oh no-they're out of town again!
Fast-ok, that's what I'll do
To get what I need-confirmation from You

What's that You say, Lord? Come
linger near?
You want to whisper in my ear!
But Lord, I'm asking for clarity
Hold on one minute and let me think.

Now, what shall I do to prove myself?
Shall I lift up my hands and beg for help?
Bow the knee and bow the head?
Present myself as though I were dead?

Excuse me Father, did I hear You speak?
I was talking there, and Your
Words were bleak.
"STOP, my child-and listen to Me!
There's only one thing from you I need.

Ready your heart and position your mouth
Dig down deep and let it out
No more thinking, you don't have to guess
You can answer My Call, by just saying, *Yes*!

Dedicated to:

They That Wait...

For those, who like me, have found

yourself in that place between your

requests to GOD, and His answers to

you-waiting patiently upon Him!

But those who wait on the Lord shall

renew their strength.

They shall mount up with wings as eagles.

They shall run and not be weary. They

shall walk and not faint

Isaiah 40:31

IN THE WAITING

Have you ever been *In The Waiting*
Seeking an answer from the Lord
Standing by with baited breath
To hear what thus saith the Lord?

Have you ever been *In The Waiting*
Hoping He heard your faintest cry
Wishing the Lord would hurry up
While knowing He'll answer by and by?

Have you ever been *In The Waiting*
Looking for Christ to come on through
Holding on tightly to your faith
Because you know what GOD can do?

Have you ever been *In The Waiting*
Feeling like you're at the end
Trying hard to keep it together
Wanting the broken parts to mend?

Have you ever been *In The Waiting*
Reaching out to understand
Though confusion makes its debut
Having done all, you continue to stand?

Have you ever been *In The Waiting*
Waiting to finally let go
Of all the hurt, pain, and sorrow
And the constant sobbing flow?

When you find you're *In The Waiting*
Know there's room at the Cross
Bring your troubles, bring your failures
Place them where Christ paid the cost.

So if you're ever *In The Waiting*
And you need a real breakthrough
Trust in GOD while you go through it
He will move mountains for you!

To:

My Lovesick Friends...

God Is Love!

We love Him because He first loved us.

1 John 4:19

NO GREATER LOVE

No greater love-Ah, yes!
No greater love made low
No greater love in all the world
No greater I know!

No greater love cast off
No greater love denied
No greater love rejected, too
No greater love that died!

No greater love protects
No greater love appeals
No greater love shed all His blood
No greater love that heals!

No greater love so rich
No greater love so pure
No greater love, to each He gives
No greater love endures!

No greater love has passed
No greater love today
No greater love for everyone
No greater love all paid!

No greater love so high
No greater love-profound
No greater love surrounding me
No greater love around!

No greater love we feel
No greater love we see
No greater love for you my friend
And, No greater love for me!

Dedicated to:

The Know-ers...

Knowing GOD'S Word has caused you to
know His Excellence!

O Lord, our Lord, how excellent is Your
name in all the earth.

Psalm 8:1a

O LORD

Your thoughts towards me are
planned, O Lord
You've paved the way for me
You've managed well my journey, Lord
Provided all my needs
You've given me a peace, O Lord
I want to linger near
You've let me see Your hand, O Lord
No longer shall I fear
You've made my hands to war, O Lord
My fingers to battle strong
Prepared my feet to walk, O Lord
And follow You along
You send Your angels daily, Lord
Your Kingdom they advance
And show me how to win, O Lord
Dear God of a second chance
You feed and strengthen me, O Lord
You never let me fall

I raise my hand to You, O Lord
You've seen me through it all
For I remember when, O Lord
I lived outside of You
Could never make it over, Lord
Until I bowed to You
So wonderful to know You, Lord
To know Your ways so pure
And for You, by you, in You Lord
Right to the end endure
Your face I'll see one day, O Lord
Can hardly wait until
But until then, I will, O Lord
Be found within your will

For:

The Peace-Seekers...

To all who know the pain of being ill at ease with life, and need to be encouraged to know there is a more excellent way.

You will keep him in perfect peace, whose
mind is stayed on You,
because he trusts in You.
Isaiah 26:3

BE AT PEACE

Be at peace, I know you can
Let GOD'S touch be in your hand
Upon your head and in your heart
Allow GOD'S quiet to impart
Talk no more, in Him be still
Prepare to do the Master's will
Stifle now, yourself...behold
As His plan to you is told
Bear within the Holy hush
Kick aside the rat race rush
For in the silence GOD will speak
Strength to you where you are weak
Comfort for your weary soul
Trade the timid for the bold
Spirit-filling words of life
Take the place of stirring strife
Manifested healing within
Because of He who knows no sin
Be still and know that He is GOD

He never slumbers, knows no nod
Stays awake that you might find
Precious rest and peace of mind
Calms your nerves, He lingers near
To whisper mercies in your ear
Extends His grace so you won't fall
But stand in faith throughout it all
A confidence you have in Him
Ever full, filled to the brim
So be refreshed, you blessed child
Camp out with Him and sit awhile
For all your worries they have ceased
You're covered by the Prince of Peace!

To:

The Unquenchable Worshippers...
You know Who life is all about!

God is Spirit, and those who worship Him

must worship in spirit and in truth.

John 4:24

YOU, GOD, YOU

Hide, GOD, Hide me in Your Wing
Press, GOD, Press me in
Praise, GOD, Praise to You I bring
Cleanse, GOD, Cleanse my sin

Mold, GOD, Mold me to Your will
Break, GOD, Break my own
Mercy, GOD, Mercy I will find
At, GOD, At Your Throne

Touch, GOD, Touch my inner man
Still, GOD, Still my heart
Reach, GOD, Reach into that place
Teach, GOD, Teach-Impart

Feed, GOD, Feed me more each day
Lead, GOD, Lead me through
Kneel, GOD, Kneel I as I pray
More, GOD, More like You

You're, GOD, You're my everything
Love, GOD, Love I You
Make, GOD, Make my lips to sing
Keep, GOD, Keep me true

Be, GOD, Be my all in all
Live, GOD, Live through me
Catch, GOD, Catch me when I fall
Raise, GOD, Raise You me!

Why, GOD, Why do You love me?
How, GOD, How so long?
Grace, GOD, Grace that set me free
Hope, GOD, Hope so strong!

Who, GOD, Who is like You, Lord?
Is, GOD, Is there none?
Not, GOD, Not in all the world
No, GOD, No not one!

To:

The Living Testimonies...
Those who can attest to knowing the beauty, privilege, and blessing of being kept by the Lord.

The Lord is your keeper: The Lord is your shade at your right hand.
Psalm 121:5

OH, TO BE KEPT BY JESUS

Oh, to be kept by Jesus
Nestled tightly in His arms of love
Guided by His ever beaming Heart Light
Reaching upward towards His face above

Oh, to be kept by Jesus
Never more to worry about a thing
Giving over every thought to Him-ward
Receive from Him a new song to sing!

Oh, to be kept by Jesus
Knowing everything is met in Christ
Gladly laying down my burdens at Him
Resting in the One who does suffice

Oh, to be kept by Jesus
Needing nothing more to solve my case
Goodness follows me wherever I go
Reaping harvest, nothing comes to waste

Oh, to be kept by Jesus

Nor to ever be left alone

God has promised never to leave me

Right beside me stay, His will be done

Oh, to be kept by Jesus

Leaning on the Everlasting Arms

Strong protector, Strong deliverer

Watching to keep me safe from all harm

Oh, to be kept by Jesus

Not encumbered with a load of care

Gleaning all I can from being with him

I run with haste to meet my Master there!

Dedicated to:

The Unfinished Ones...

Finding it hard to move along sometimes?

Just know you are still

"In Production"!

*And not only that, but we also glory in
tribulations, knowing that tribulation
produces perseverance; and perseverance,
character; and character, hope.*

Romans 5:3-4

PERSEVERE

*Persevere, keep on, don't stop-Just run this
race with grace
Travel long and follow hard, though
obstacles you face
Press on through and hang on to, be strong
and carry on
Count your trials as blessings, and make
victory your song
Push on past them that oppose the task
placed in your hand
Trusting GOD no matter what-When all else
fails, just stand
Get a grip, go forth with grit-Hold on to Who
you know
GOD will tell you when to move and show
you where to go
Tired? Catch the Glory Train! It's always
passing by*

Providing rest along the way-Sit down!

Enjoy the ride!

Look to the hills

That's where your help is coming from,

my friend

Peer right into the eyes of Christ, He'll lead

you 'til the end

It's not by power, nor by might

Don't get me wrong...He's strong!

But it's by His Holy Spirit He will move you

right along

So, capture all your thoughts

And build a fence around your plans

Now pick them up and turn them over

To the Master's hands!

Here's a question posed to every heart that reads these words...

Do you have "ACCESS" to the King?

Through Whom also we have access by faith into this grace in which we stand, and rejoice in hope of the Glory of GOD.

Romans 5:2

DO YOU HAVE ACCESS
TO THE KING?

Do you have access to the King of Glory?
Do you have favor with GOD your King?
Can you be sure He'll come when
you call him?
Will you forever His praises sing?

Do you know Jesus, our Lord and
our Savior?
Have you met Christ, our redeemer
and Friend?
Did you know faith is the way to
the Kingdom?
Are you ready a victory to win?

For salvation is free but not cheap-Christ
paid for it
On Calvary's Cross, where He hung,
bled, and died

Then laid in a tomb, but He didn't
stay laid there
Rose up with all power, and death
was denied!

GOD'S perfect plan to draw us straight
to Him
For man couldn't do what was
needed to live
And bring Himself under the
Master's Authority
So Christ gave His life-what more
could He give?

He gave up the precious for our filthy rags
But now holds the key to our future success
He's building His Kingdom with
those who will let Him
And those who submit to GOD'S
Will as their best

It doesn't take long to cross over to Him
The bridge has been made-It's strong,
it will hold
GOD's Son is that bridge, Christ Jesus,
The Life-line
Come quickly to meet Him! Come running,
come bold!

So, has anyone told you there's
mansions awaiting?
In heaven for you if you'll trust Him today?
Confess your sins and believe GOD
will save you
Then open the door and let GOD
have His way!

To:

All the FAMILIES of the World...

The first institution created and
established by GOD,
to show His character of unconditional
love and unity.

*"At the same time," says the Lord, "I will be
the GOD of all the families of Israel,
and they shall be my people."*
Jeremiah 31:1

FAMILY

GOD'S Idea

Man and Woman

Husband and Wife

Soul and Spirit

Commit and Concede

Bear and Believe

Parents and Children

Hustle and Bustle

Do's and Don'ts

Ups and Downs

Fathers and Daughters

Teach and Know

Mothers and Sons

Grasp and Grow

Brothers and Sisters

Give and Take

Generation to Generation

Build and Break

Legacy and Integrity

Young and Old

Experience and Example

Shy and Bold

Strengths and Weaknesses

Failures and Triumphs

Joy and Sorrow

Victory and Defeat

Death and Life

Love and Hate

War and Peace

GOD'S Idea

FAMILY

To:

The Reflectors...

When life shatters the image of you,

it's time to see yourself in the

image of GOD.

I will praise You, for I am fearfully and

wonderfully made;

Marvelous are your works, and that my

soul knows very well.

Psalm 139:14

I SEE MYSELF AGAIN

Looking in the mirror of life
I look myself again

Through the eyes of pain and strife
I see myself again

Glancing at the sky above
I watch myself again

Fixing on the distant dove
I fix myself again

Reaching up beyond my reach...
I reach myself again

"Fore times taught that I may teach
I teach myself again

Once bewildered and confused
I clear myself again

Wretched, weary, worn, and used
Refresh myself again

Couldn't stand, all strength was gone
I stand myself again

Pain-riddled, helpless bones
I build myself again

Hands upraised-I said, "I'm out!"
Begin myself again

Condemned, prejudged, and talked about
Reprieved myself again

Forgotten, cast off, left for dead
I live myself again

A hungry soul, let me be fed
I feed myself again

Dismal grief, the darkness thick
I breathe myself again

Light is dim, goes out the wick
I light myself again

Roots dried up, so withered and bruised,
I grow myself again

Rejected, abandoned, and abused
I heal myself again

Once sequestered, pushed away
I find myself again

Outcast, thrown out, put at bay
Include myself again

Scrub-a-dub, O filth be gone
I clean myself again

Got a friend, won't be alone
I glean myself again

Walk me through that open door
I walk myself again

Ministry, come 'round once more
I preach myself again

Examined, found to be undone
I fill myself again

Now, I'm the vindicated one
I'm free, myself, again

Dedicated to:

The Few...

Who after many trials of thought, have
come to know the power of a renewed
mind in Christ.

*And do not be conformed to this world, but
be transformed by the renewing of your
mind, that you may prove what is that good
and acceptable and perfect will of GOD.*
Romans 12:2

I WOULD BE INSANE, LORD

*I would be insane, Lord, not to want to
touch You
Your touch is the most awesome thing I know
You have been more to me than anyone else
In the earth, or in heaven above
I know that there is none like You
If these were my last moments alive
I'd scurry to spend them with You...alone
I love You that much, Lord
You continue to hold me close to You
Your hugs take me away inside of you
Hiding in Your shadows
I find my strength and my song
Your Ruach breath resuscitates me
Moment by precious moment
My heart is filled with Your goodness
My voice, it's filled with Your praise
You are my Life-blood, Holy Spirit
Nestled safely under the wings of Your love*

You protect and cover my being

You are my ancient and right-now friend

You, alone, are always there for me

How can I be there for You, O Tower

of Refuge?

I stand on my knees to pour me out before

You

I drink from your well that never runs dry

O Fountain of Waters, I thirst completely

for You

You have never lied to me-Your truth has

set me free

I don't remember my life without You

I just cannot recall

The wave of Your hand has swept me

The power of Your love has kept me

Just to be close to You-for a moment,

for an hour

That's all I ever need

Every second of every minute

My thoughts are consumed of You, my GOD

You are a fortress for me, O Mighty One
I am always safe in You, with You, by You,
through You
I never let a day go by without praising
Your name
What shall I render unto GOD for all
His blessings?
I know that there is none like you
You have been more to me that
everyone else
In the earth or in the heavens above
Yes, I would be insane, Lord-not to want
to touch You

To:

All of the *"Geeks"* for GOD...

A first-ministry admonishment to my
fellow-laborers in the Lord!

*And whatever you do, do it heartily, as to
the Lord and not to men, knowing that from
the Lord you will receive the reward of the
inheritance: for you serve the Lord CHRIST.*
Colossians 3:23-24

MAKE GOD YOUR HOME PAGE

Make Him the first *Site* you see
each morning
Make GOD your Home Page
Make Him the *Point* to start from each day
Make GOD your Home Page
Make Him the *Access* you go through
each evening
Make GOD your Home Page
Make Him the *Portal* that guides your way
Make GOD your Home Page
Make Him the *All-in-One Stop* to halt at
Make GOD your Home Page
Make Him your *Server Directory Lead*
Make GOD your Home Page
Make Him the *Local File* you click into
Make GOD your Home Page
Make him the *All Day Mail* that you read
Make GOD your Home Page

Make Him the *Front*, the *Feature*,

the *Focus*

Make GOD your Home Page

Make Him the *Storage* your memory holds

Make GOD your Home Page

Make Him the *Place* you set all your

affections

Make GOD your Home Page

Make Him the *Engine* that searches

your soul

Make God your Home Page

To:

The Speakers...

A spoken word for you-written that you
might allow GOD to sketch-draw this
image of His sacrifice in your heart...then
use you to reveal His heavenly mural
to a dying world.

For God so loved the world that He gave
His only begotten Son, that whoever
believes in Him should not perish but
have everlasting life.
John 3:16

PICTURE THIS

A tense sky against the backdrop of a
rocky mountain
The breath of the waters cease at the
wonder to come
The clouds turn aside from their gathering
to await
Anticipation of greatness hits the air
The trees bend forward to hear the
rumor whispers
Darkness prepares to make its
unwelcome entrance
The thunder steals away to practice
its eventful clap
The sun slowly bends the knee, rehearsing
his fateful fall
As the moon dips its form and
brightness in blood
Ready to afflict and affront are the
driver's tools

Cords of affliction break and fetter the
flesh of Humility
Men of unaware surround the foot of the
place of Redemption
While blood-filled drops shower those
prospects below
The power of persuasion
Captivates and arouses the un-awakened
And rocks, unable to grasp the gaul
Tremble at the sheer horror of the moment
A deafening sound vibrates throughout
the Giver's territory
The liar's laugh lurks in the shadows
To mock and to call out
And the green grass growing all around
and around
The green grass smiling...makes a frown
Who can comprehend the thought of a King
Who dies for His subjects?
An edict written in Blood for any to receive

The unworthy, unthankful,

unregenerate, unaffected

Dust-man

Oblivious to the power of the Cross-

Shaped surrender

Unscathed by the shakedown for the

takedown in the heavens

Puppets unaware of the puppeteer's

true identity

Molding and manipulating the clueless

beings at-will

To kill, steal, mame, and destroy

What he knows to be the Son of

The Living GOD

Yet, the underbelly of death, cut asunder

and torn to shreds

Nauseates the earthly hole

So that the grave must yield its meal

Ah, what Light in yonder window breaks?

It is Life Revealed and Truth Returned!

Hey, Hey, Hey...What ya' got to say?

Hallelu...Hallelujah!
Colors, numbers, symbols, signs
Can you picture all of this in the recesses
of your minds?
To the heart of faith, it's a mural of bliss
But, can you handle the Love?
Can you picture this?

What's In A Name?

A Compilation of Prophetic Utterings and Heartfelt Encouragements

GOD has taken the time, love, and painstaking efforts to name us all. Each one of us has been issued a name to live by. Some of us are aware of our names and their power, while others have yet to explore the profound nature and origin of their name. Our name identifies us in many ways. None of us are faceless, nameless beings. We all have value and importance. We matter to GOD.

These next few pages are prophetic encouragements given to a few, amongst the many, gifted and special persons who are impacting the Kingdom of GOD by living out the true meaning of their GOD-Given name and call.

Dedicated to:

My Precious Mother...

I remember hearing you pray for me. That remembrance of you impacted my life at age 19. I love you, Mom.

Charm is deceitful and beauty is passing,
But a woman who fears the Lord,
she shall be praised.
Proverbs 31:30

I LIVE BECAUSE
MAMA PRAYED

Since I was brought into this world
When I was just a little girl
She'd wipe my tears and calm my fears
I live Because Mama Prayed.

When I look back on things I've done
Now I look at what I've become
Mama's been there to say a prayer
I Live Because Mama Prayed.

In this world of yes and no
Of up and down, of to and fro
I stand today to let you know
I Live Because Mama Prayed.

Want to know about my life
Of little worry, pain, or strife
Want to know what I know is right
I Live Because Mama Prayed.

If I could write a storybook
About my life and what it took
To raise up me, the title would be
I Live Because Mama Prayed.

To:

The Cassandra's of this world...

Defender of man, Fearless Warrior

Prophetic Gift You Are

Inflamed with My Love, I extinguish you not.

I will watch you burn with Holy Fire.

*For you understand Me-you ride the waves
of faith on My behalf.*

You are for Me, My Lady.

*I am your defense, and you are Mine.
You trust Me.*

Thank you for accepting the call

*To be unheeded, ignored-An ambassador
of standing.*

As your cheer turns to compassion

And your laughter to mourning-I
meet you there.

Oh prophetic gift you are

I will cause men to hear Me through you

And be helped, changed, lifted, encouraged

Made better by My Strength and your song

I will not be ignored through you

"I Will Be Heard", says the Lord Most High

Call on me, O fearless one

Start with Me, for I love your voice

Tell it to me-I love to listen!

I will press in to grasp what your heart wants to express.

I know your heart-It resembles Mine.

With it I am quite familiar. Our hearts beat as one.

I've shaped and formed you as My Warrior That's My Sword you carry in your heart and your hand

Never let it go, for it is useful to you

To keep you grounded, unfettered, and true

Just like Me, you see.

A watchman on the wall...up there by yourself a lot, aren't you?

Good lookin' out, for I have strategically placed you there.

Grumble not. Murmur not. For I have not forsaken you.

You see much from My Special Standpoint

Just give what you see back to me

Believe Me, I got it! I can handle it! It's My Fight!

I just need you to be right...

Right where you belong-singing my song

Chirping for me, while I set men free

Sing a song to stop the sting

And raise your hands, the victory I'll bring!

See, your hope is in what I say, not what you feel

I know it can be hard, but don't forget to P.U.S.H.

I'm holding you, O Kingdom cryer

Cry out for the little ones, the down-trodden, the forgotten

Cry with your sweet chords unto me

Remember I Come! I Hear! I Do! I Reign!

Defender of man…Prophetic gift… Fearless warrior

Live out your name, in My Name!

To:

GOD'S Gwen's...
fair, white, blessed, holy

DAUGHTER OF MY HOLINESS

Hmm...got a minute? Can you spare
some time?

I need you now!

Let's talk about this thing, together

In one place, at one time

There is a fairness about you that works.

It's hidden sometimes, but it's there. I put
it there.

It's because of Me that you operate fairly.

Your name expresses this.

You are a blessing to me, child.

I just wanted you to hear this from Me.

I have loved you for so long, and
forever will.

Do you think it fair that I chose you?

Some say favor isn't fair...

Who is the originator of that thought?
Not Me.

Favor has always been fair in my eyes

I grant to whom I may. Always have.
Always will.

Back to your name...

There is a clearness about you that you
don't see

Others see it as white, but it is clear.

I will reveal this to you in My
Time-stay open.

You are Holy, Gwen.

Your name has holiness attached to it.
You are righteous through My Son

His sacrifice has made you that way to Me.

It is a cool, calm, and collected walk I have
entrusted to you.

It is of Me.

As you use the time and resources
I give you

To teach others fullness and peace

Know that I will replenish what you
expend on My behalf.

You recognize lack and hate it-just like
Me.

This is why I use you like I do.

I am taking back daily what the enemy
steals

From Me and My people.

Focus on me while you go, for I teach you
as you move.

You will not falter or flutter. You will not
bend nor break.

You will not be shaken or moved.

You understand, and I am thrilled!

Happy you are to see the Kingdom built
from within

And you have your part.

Stay the course-You are being watched.

There are those who will come after you

You will be positioned

To pass the mantle of blessing on to them
like a lit torch.

But for now, hold it up high with your
words of life

Daughter of My Holiness!

You Are My Rose

ROSE

Hello, garden of My loveliness!
I awaken you to Me!
How beautiful you are!
I blanketed you at night with My warmth.
I covered you in My care.

It's feeding time, My dear!
Feast 'til your heart's content from My table.
Then, we will proceed.

I planted you long ago for such a time as this.
My, how you have grown!
I place your feet on the mountains.
You tread the mountains for Me.
Oh, how I trust you!

You are My personal flower.
Your scent is My fragrance in you!
You let me cultivate you often

My pruning has become your desire
Oh, how you trust Me!

Even though I pluck and scatter your parts
Amongst the field
Still you thrive and flourish.
Although I crush you as I teach you
Yet, you remain in My Will.
You make Me famous!

Your strength is furious. Your resolve is total.
Your faith is pure. You are for Me!

Much have I given to you.
Much have I required of you.
You are not a Rose by any other name!
Drink from My waters to quench your thirst
Let me refresh your fatigued soul!

Receive from my Light your full illumination
I choose to enlighten your way as I have
promised.
I am your soil and your air!

I breathe through you
That you may color your surroundings.
For you are My precious Bouquet.
You are My Rose!

To every Tamiko & Tamika out there...

Your name says you are GOD's Benefit,

for others to see.

Let Them See

You have been made to let them see

The marvelous works I've created in thee

You do exist as My pure light

I shine through you-It's My delight!

I ever know the path you take

My promise to you, I will not break.

To put you out there, for My Good

To cover you with My Great Hood

But do not fret, transparent one

I've paired you strongly with My Son

Together you will trample over

Death, demise, deceit-and more!

Be not afraid, Stay in My hand

I'll take you where no other can!

And use you richly-Use you up!

Come dine with Me-Let's drink and sup!

Be strengthened for the road ahead

Let me stay up-Go back to bed!

Then rise and know as you have before

How I'm for you-Your Open Door
You don't forget Me-I like that!

That's why I placed you where I'm at

We move as one, We do agree

It's great to have you here with Me!

I'll warn you, child-It's all good, now

But up the road, you'll wonder how

And why the way has twists and turns

*And scars and bumps and bruises
and burns*

Your rubbings, though, will tell a tale

How through it all, still Me you hail!

That even when you feel alone

You'll trust in Me, Who's on the Throne

So there you have it, So now you know

I've favored you-You are My Show!

All that you are will flame for Me

And folks will come from miles to see

To picture you in glorious array

While in My arms, I let you lay

My Skin you're in, and you're made to fit

'Cause girl, You are God's Benefit!

Sheila...

Whoever and wherever you are

Your Prince Speaks!

My Love For You

Sheila...I love you so much!

I have always loved you

From before the foundations of the world

were laid

I have known you. I created you in My love.

I purposed you in Love

I fashioned you in My Image

According to My Great Love

I built you painstakingly, from My Heart

of Love

I blew My breath into you

Out of the Love I have for you

My Love has raised you, kept you

Made you to be so much like Me in all

your ways

Know this, Sheila...even your name

reminds Me

Of My total Love for you

A gentle, blind, woman of GOD...ready to
be poured into
Gentle, you are, just like My nature
Blind, you are, so I can always be
your guide
Woman, you are, so that I'll always
have a bride
Yes, Sheila...I have fond memories of you
You've made me smile and laugh
So much, in your lifetime
I've had a ball so far, with you, My Lovely
But I have more Love to shower upon you
More Love than you could ever imagine!
Receive My Love, dear one! Let me lavish
you with it always!
Take My Love, precious one! Let me
drench you in it always!
For there will never be one who will Love
you like I do
I am jealous for you, Sheila
I trust only Myself with this Great Love

You are in My Heart. You are in My Hand.

I will not release you from My Grip. You
mean that much to Me.

So just settle in and let me do it...I will do
it for awhile.

For the picture of you brings joy to Me.

Let My Deep Love flood your soul, even to
overflowing

I am choked up by the beauty of you

My light shines through you

Sheila...sweet on My lips! Always fresh on
My Mind!

I think of you often as I perform My
Marvelous Works!

You are one of them...My Child, My
Daughter, My Friend.

You are in My Spirit...I breathe your
fragrance daily.

I wake you to My Presence to refresh you.

You got it like that!

Do you want to know what your GOD is
feeling right now?
He is feeling you!
Your longings, your desires, your dreams
"How excited I am for you!," says GOD.
I am here to fulfill you, and bring you to a
realized state
But right now, won't you sit a spell? Relax
in my favor.
For as much as you know it's all about Me
I share with you...so it's about you, too!

*This has been a note of love from your
Father up above.*

Yvette, the Beautiful,...

"GOD is Merciful"

Mercy To Me

Beautiful to me are your feet, *Daughter
of Excellence!*
You walk My Way.
I have showed you My Mercy.
I love to lead you through.
My Creative Originality is nestled within
your spirit.
You carry My artistic flow.
Compassionate like Me-Charitable
and free.
You are My kind of friend, My Lady!
I built a strong determination in you
And a peaceful resilience that lets Me
through.
You have influence. *Use it to My Glory.*
Give Me the credit always.
Your eccentric flair warms Me.
Your passion and humor is alive to Me.
At My Mercy, you listen attentively.

And though independent, you depend
on Me.
You bless Me, child!
A spontaneous planner-How can that be?
Believe Me, only I know how! *I'll*
tell you later.
I am pleased at your everlasting inquiries.
You inquire of me often. Never stop.
You are My Conservative Operative
Responsible, careful, conventional,
civilized, sound.
You remind Me so much of Myself.
That's just how I wanted it to be with you!
I love you like crazy-*with your high-*
achieving self!
Remain tactful in me.
My sensitivity I find in you.
I rely on this for the ministry I have called
you to.
How imaginative I've made you

Your innovation evades and confounds-*But I know...*

And now, I implore you

Let my quiet strength command your mornings

And allow My Thoughts to guide your days. I will be seen in you.

Be at peace, My easy-going, free-spirited pawn. Be at peace.

For My Mercy calls to the depths of you

To settle you securely in My Unfathomable Peace.

To my youngest son Sean...

In your life-long search for Absolute Truth
in all things, know this...
You are a very peculiar creation of GOD.
The Lord has made you for such a time
as this. He birthed you into this world
through this Word...

*This was the Lord's doing; it is
marvelous in our eyes.*
Psalm 118:23

YOUNG MAN

Do you really know *who* you are,
young man?
You were bought with a price
Through GOD'S own Hand

You have the wealth of the
world at your feet
It's within your power, the
enemy to beat

You were made from the dust
And formed from the ground
But the breath of GOD has you
moving around

Long before your seed was sown
And well before your name was known

You were fearfully and
wonderfully made
And within your heart, GOD'S
Plan was laid

Your GOD-Given gifts will make
room for you
To fulfill His Vision, all your
life through

Deep in your spirit, GOD'S Will
you possess
To live out your dreams, and
have good success

For your righteousness is from
Christ above
He's entrusted you with His Great Love

To spread His Joy and heed His Call
Make others know, he's your All-in-All

Wake up from your slumber
and recognize
It's time to rise from your sleep-Arise!
Take up your cross and follow along
Don't let anything steer you wrong

Be bold, Be strong...Stand up for Him!
Who keeps you from falling, again
and again!

For there's healing for you in the palm
of His hand
Do you really know *Whose* you are,
young man?

A note of remembrance for my brother Michael Randolph, whom we affectionately call "Randy"...

Who since the age of nine has been plagued with severe epilepsy...traumatic episodes meant to kill him, but today he still stands through it all as a believer in Christ with a host of testimonies about GOD'S Loving Care and Protection.

ODE TO RANDY

It ain't easy being me

All I want to be is free

Unrestricted, Unrestrained

Free from bondage, Free from pain

It ain't easy, what I do

Live like this, and still be cool

Taking suffering all in stride

Still won't take away my pride

It ain't easy, looking this way

Mouth all wired and nerves all frayed

Tubes and needles everywhere

Open-robed and bottom-bare

It ain't easy, you just try

To hang on tight-hold in that cry

Trade me, then we'll both agree

That it ain't easy being me.

A Special Note about our Children

Did you know that there is no *Jr.* Holy
Spirit? There is no *"smaller"* GOD to tell
our children about. We must teach our
children about The One True GOD...the
same GOD that we as adults believe in
and serve. GOD trusts children with
a whole lot more than we many times
give them credit for. And even though
children are playful, can be cute, are
diverse in their nature, and tend to imitate
their parents...we must remember that
children are separate individual beings,
who are capable of things like glorifying

GOD with their lives, coming to Christ, understanding scripture, receiving the promises of GOD, having belief, being trained, and worshiping in GOD'S House.

The Bible records many illustrations of children, like Joseph, Samuel, David, Esther, and Jesus, who were obedient, respectful, anointed, gifted, and called by GOD...and were able to do great and mighty works that were pleasing to GOD.

Likewise, the same Bible gives us examples of *"bad kids"* like the sons of Eli, Absalom, and the 42 children who mocked the prophet Elisha...these children chose to be rebellious and had to suffer the consequences for their hellish ways.

After serving in ministry to children for over 20 years now, some of my greatest joys have come in seeing children pray openly...at the altar, prayer walking, on their knees, at their seats...If you've never been in the presence of the Lord as He is ministering to children that way, you have missed a treat!

Teaching children to talk to and listen to GOD through prayer and meditation is key. We must train them to be prayer operatives...to know and use GOD'S actual Word in prayer-strategically.

We can't be afraid that we are overwhelming and inundating our children with too much of **GOD**. I assure you, the media, arts, and entertainment industries have thought it through. They make it a daily point to inundate and overwhelm your children with sounds, smells, and images...designed to capture their attention while young and impressionable, and eventually positioning them as far away from the mindset of Christ as possible. We have to be proactive about reaching our children and establishing a strong foundation in them for Godliness.

Children **need** to know their Creator. They **need** to know that their One True GOD loves them and has a cool plan for their life! They **need** to know they are sinners and can do no good thing to save themselves from sin. They **need** to know that Christ died for their sin, to save them from hell. They **need** to know that the only way to Heaven is to accept Christ as their Savior and Lord. They **need** to know that salvation means they now have permission to *not have* to sin! They **need** to know that God can use them to build His Kingdom!

These are things we must not
keep from children.

GOD is holding us as the parents,
guardians, shepherds, and mentors of
these children, responsible for pouring
in to them what He has instructed for us
to. We are without excuse, and will come
under GOD'S Judgement for disobedience,
if we fail to do so.

You already have what you need to get
started. Life, the Bible, your children,
today...don't let these precious moments
pass you by. Make it your life commitment
to sow into a child's life by introducing
them to an Awesome GOD!

A CHILD'S PRAYER DECLARATION

Even a child is known by his doings;
whether his work be pure, and
whether it be right.
Proverbs 20:11

O Great GOD, How I praise you, Lord
You're everything I need
You sent to me this beautiful day
A wondrous gift I see!

I thank you for your Only Son
Who gave me liberty
Christ Jesus is His Holy name
The one who died for me!

I really love my friend, dear GOD
Who gave His life away
He hung and bled on Calvary's Cross
That I might live today!

I do accept the Savior's Love
Forgiving me of sin
Forgetting all the bad I did
Now I can make it in!

I won't forget Your Promise, Lord
To always be with me
And teach me all your perfect ways
So I can follow Thee!

I need Your help, so help me please
Do goodness in Your sight
I do not want to stumble
For I want to walk upright!

Another thing You promised
That you'd give me right away
Is Your Holy, Righteous Spirit
He will guide me through each day!

And show me how to tell the world
About your darling Son
Who freed the world by His own blood
And now Salvation's won!

The devil can't have me no more
I've quit playing his games
Because I gave my heart to you
I'll never be the same!

So as I grow in grace, My GOD
And live in victory
I'll glorify Your name each day
In You, I've been set free!

CPSIA information can be obtained
at www.ICGtesting.com
Printed in the USA
BVHW081729121022
649284BV00003B/503